Copyright © 2022 Charles Levien
All rights reserved.
ISBN: 978-1-9163777-5-2

Cover from an oil painting 'Light on Fields'
by Maggie Levien

Another View

Charles Levien

Dedication

For Judy, my best friend and life's companion.

About the Poet

When I was young, we lived in what was termed the green belt; an attempt to limit the inevitable expansion of London suburbs. Behind our house, across a playing field, was a playground of neglected land overgrown with rough grass — a boggy area we called 'the swamp' and a small stream which bordered a golf course.

This "other world" was, for a moment, in the 1950's, a place for exploration and my first contact with the natural world. Looking back, I see that it was as formative as anything learned in the classroom because it gave me a sense of adventure. I subsequently went on to travel in Africa, riding horses around a sugar plantation and a motorbike around a tobacco farm. I learned to speak in the local vernacular, a sort of Lingua Franca of Southern Africa: a language full of onomatopoeia, though not so useful in the leafy lanes of England, to which I returned in 1969.

Work as an Outward Bound instructor in Scotland followed, and marriage to my life's companion, Judy. Then came the years of responsibility, running a business to pay for a mortgage and feed a growing family of three.

I "retired" at sixty and time flew by until the first Covid lockdown arrived, out of the blue. For seven months my wife and I lived in a small barn we had built in an area of woodland, planted by us in 1991 — the trees now big enough to walk beneath.

We read a lot, enjoyed walking together and I started writing poetry, seeing the natural world again as though through the eyes of that child that discovered it once before. But now I saw how we are part of the natural world and how it may relate to our humanity. Some of my poems verge towards the romantic and I do identify with Wordsworth's line, "The child is father of the man." I prefer, "The child is father to the man", but I'm not going to misquote that great man here.

In this small book of poems, you will find some simple heartfelt words where questions seem more important than answers.

September 2022

Contents

Harvest 11

Woodland Cabin 13

A Late November Day 15

When You Are Gone 17

Anybody's Hand 19

Autumn Colours 21

Jude at Eighteen Months 23

Some Candles.. 25

Mother Dear 27

It Is As Well.. 29

Blackberrying 31

Another View.. 33

Barbara Hepworth.. 35

On the Beach 39

St Mawes... 41

New Beginnings 43

It's Just Not Cricket 45

Saving the Planet... 47

April First 49

A Numpty.. 51

Standing at the Gate...................................... 53

But Not from School 55

Caught Out.. 57

A Tree Near Here.. 59

Nuances... 61

So Many Ways to Fall... 63

Love Is 65

A Christmas Card 67

A Doggy Conundrum 69

Haiku 2022 71

The River Babingley... 73

Stiffkey Marshes... 75

Acknowledgments... 77

Notes on Harvest:

There is something about handwriting; instantly recognisable, familiar, a letter perhaps or an old family recipe. In this case, it is my wife's pencilled notes on some brown paper packets of seed she had recently collected from the garden.

Harvest

High summer. Stubble in the fields.
And in the garden, flowers, gone to seed.
The lanes, covered with wind-blown dust
And fractured straw, left by huge machines
That moved, inexorably, across the land.

And on the kitchen table, flower seed in paper packets.

Escalonia, various colours.
Astrantia, ruby-red, white.
Meconopsis cambrica, Welsh Poppy, tangerine.
Euphorbia, milky sapped, bright green.
Carefully gathered and written in her familiar hand.

Notes on Woodland Cabin:

An early poem, from the first lockdown when we were all (well, nearly all) feeling confined by Covid and wondering if a more normal world would ever return.

Woodland Cabin

Spring came late this year, kept waiting
At summer's door by chilling winds
And rain that puddled on the woodland floor.

Then, almost imperceptibly, the trees
Began to green and woodland life, impatient,
Seen to move again.

Cabined in this wood we lovers lay
Listening to the barking deer and restless owls
Seeking mates, quite unaware of this,
Our second Covid year.

Then summer came, with open doors
And open shirts — with flowers in the meadow
That stunned the eye with scintillating brilliance.

Now the mauve of knapweed draws butterflies,
Sublime yet anxious occupiers of space and time.
The young faun hiding, ears just seen above the grass,
Alert to sound.
And I, standing silent in the passing moment,
Beauty found.

Notes on A Late November Day:

One day my wife said to me, "I wish you'd look at me when you speak to me." I'd obviously fallen into a bad habit. That phrase stuck and led to this poem.

A Late November Day

A late November day, the thinning
Hedgerows clinging to the last
Of autumn's leaves.
We walked apart, yet joined
In thought by those things
Common to us both.

Married now for fifty years,
In fact, a little more, we didn't
Need to speak. We knew
that words, like violets
Hiding under woodland trees,
Come slowly into view.

Look at me when you have
Something that you want to say.

When words come into view —
I looked at you and saw
That I am more myself
For knowing you.

Notes on When You Are Gone:

*After I read this poem to a group someone came up to me and said,
"It's not like that at all."*

When You Are Gone

Shall I still hear your voice
When you depart?
And if I do, I shall reply,
Of all the people I have known
You are the one
That truly held my heart.

Should I be less alone
If I could say those simple words
We used to greet each other
At the start of each new day.

Notes on Anybody's Hand:

It is so sad and seems so preposterous now that husbands, wives, sons, daughters could not be together in those last moments of life in intensive care. I hope it is comforting to know that someone, a nurse, a doctor, was there at the end to simply hold a hand.

Anybody's Hand

Can I lose you if I truly love you?
For if I love you, and I do,
The memory of those times we had
Together, will keep you ever
In my heart.

But what if memories fade,
Are harder to recall, are left behind?
Then I shall hold a hand, anybody's
Hand. It will be yours.
It will be mine.

Notes on Autumn Colours:

I wrote this after seeing trees buffeted in a full gale of wind, at a point of transition from Autumn to Winter. It's about acceptance of inevitable change and loss, but finding redemption in the prospect of renewal.

Autumn Colours

Sometimes words come slow
Like colour seeping into autumn leaves.
The leaving sun betrays the green
Of summer until we see a memory
Of its warmth in amber hues
That crown the roadside trees.

Then come the autumn gales
That strip the trees of colour.
Like a tall ship, slow to shorten canvas,
The tall trees, flailing in a storm of sound,
Lose the Midas touch and leave
Their gold upon the ground.

And so my life it seems is much
Like this. Those fleeting days
Of youth, betrayed by time.
Until the passing years leave memories behind
And children, with their children,
The golden leaves that shine.

Notes on Jude at Eighteen Months:

In Eden still, a place of happy childhood before the strictures that inevitably come with growing up.

Jude at Eighteen Months

Oh! Jude, Jude, Jude, what is the skill
That captivates us so? In Eden still
And innocently deaf to No. A triumph
In every smiling moment.
Your rocking gait as down the hall you go.

Asleep through summer mornings, the birds
Outside teaching their young to fly.
Then awake you hear the sound of mother's voice
Beside your cot and see her arms held wide.

What would I say to you, as you explore
Your toys, still strewn cross the playroom floor?
I'd simply say, enjoy your life.
The plans you make, the path you take,
Whatever lies in store.

Notes on Some Candles:

I was looking after our youngest grandchild, Jude. She wanted to show me something as we walked through Heydon. I felt a little tug on my hand as we approached the church.

Some Candles

Today, we went into the village church,
My granddaughter and I. With lifted latch
The dark, oak door eased open to our push.
I am nearly eighty, she is barely
Two, and yet she took my hand and led me
Past the upright empty pews, the polished
Flagstone floor.

She took me to a stained glass window.
The morning light shone through the image
Of a mother and child. In Memoriam,
It says. And on a table set before,
A taper with some candles, one alight.
I held her hand and carefully we
Lit three more.

Notes on Mother Dear:

This poem is autobiographical. What a long word to say that it's about me. I was that child and for many years found difficulty in talking about this episode in my life.

Mother Dear

Mother Dear, if I could be with you again
We could talk about those things
That caused us pain when both of us were young.
I would share the thoughts that I withheld before.
About the tears that wouldn't come when I
Was stunned by separation from your warm
Embrace, your smiling face that shone on me
Through all those wartime years.

That sad, unhappy little boy. At four years old,
Too young to understand. The child I hid
When I came back to you. I would
Hold your hand and wipe away your tears
And share with you that little boy that now
Can simply say, "I love you, Mother Dear."

Notes on It Is As Well:

Written after hearing someone say, 'It is as well' about something. The phrase stuck in my mind. I wrote it down and this poem followed. It's a love poem really.

It Is As Well

It is as well I did not know the days
That lay ahead, when hedgerows greened and Queen
Anne's lace made shy the village names.
For in that space between the winter grey
And coming summer's green, you left me. There
To see alone, through tear-filled eyes, the paths
We walked before and where we stood and saw
The shining bluebells carpeting the ground.

Can I still be sad, now that songful June
Is here again? Germander Speedwell blues
The lane as berries tint the Hawthorn trees.
I am glad we walked this wood together
And though my heart is yet to heal, I find
Some consolation in these memories.

Notes on Blackberrying:

To me, my father was a stranger when he returned to the family after the war. It was a difficult adjustment for him, too. He had been piloting a Catalina flying boat far into the North Atlantic, looking for the enemy submarines that were such a menace to our convoys. I think I was a little in awe of him, but I do remember a day when he took me out to pick blackberries. He was a countryman at heart.

Blackberrying

When I was four years old, my father took
Me blackberrying. I remember how
We crossed a field of autumn grass that brushed
My knees and wet my khaki shorts, and there
Were pats of crusted brown where cows had been.

We reached a hedge where he'd seen a good place
To begin. How high he seemed to reach
To get the brightest fruit. This man, my father
A tall stranger, home from war.

My father seems now closer to my heart.
He died some years ago, but in my thoughts
He came with me again today when I
Went blackberrying, remembering that day
He held my hand and wanted me to see
The boy within the man.

Notes on Another View:

Here I contrast the ease of changing the landscape with a chainsaw against an older pre-industrial age, when manpower and horses did the slow, hard work. Life is easier now, but something has been lost.

Another View

We took out an old piece of hedge today.
A morning's work, with chainsaw, tractor
And the two of us pulling out the dead wood.
The hedge was thin and we will plant another
Line of greening hawthorn where it stood.

Through the gap, we could see the tower
Of the parish church, standing out against the pale
Grey January sky. Five hundred years
Have passed since this was built, with lime and sand,
By hands that wiped away the cold wind tears.

The walls are faced with flint. Knapped and shaped
Then carefully placed with little space between.
Impervious to rain and wind.
Built to last forever. Set in its wall
A clock; once the arbiter of village time.

Five centuries ago, a man and horse
Would sweat to plough an acre in a day.
He worked the land, the only life he knew.
The church for him a welcome day of rest.
For some today, it's just another view.

Notes on Barbara Hepworth:

*After visiting her cottage and studio at St Ives and seeing the
excellent exhibition there of her work and life, I was left with a feeling of
sadness. This may not be a true reflection of what she felt at the time, but
I imagine there might have been a conflict between the pressure of work and
the demands of motherhood.*

Barbara Hepworth

We parked at Carbis Bay
Then walked across the sand
Towards St Ives.
On our right, the early morning light
Reflected from a watercolour sky
Of pink, upon a distant haze of blue.

Then came those steps that rise
As though cut from the rock,
A sort of mounting block before
We topped this ancient spur
That sits secure above the sand.

We searched for Hepworth's cottage,
The one she bought before the tourists
Crammed these narrow streets.
Before the coffee stops, the shops
With tablet fudge and sweets.

On the left just past the church, yes,
That's the place where Barbara Hepworth lived.
A few more steps then through a door and here's
Another world, another time.
The story of a woman's life, her loves,
Her losses, her energy unceasing
Despite the human cost.

Her studio, as she left it, expecting to be back.
The tall white marble waiting for the black
Paint brush upon a pole that deftly makes
The mark, the place to start.

But in the garden, ringed by trees,
There stands a piece in hollow bronze
That sings when gently tapped by
Knuckled hand. It's shape
A treasured pebble from the beach.

But look inside, it's hollow. And through
The back, three holes, as if the sea
Has scoured out this shape and made
A perfect pool, refreshed by rain
That gently drains through one to keep
It's perfect shape.

These three holes: are they the triplets
She had to give away to others' care?
This pool of water, her tears which now,
Refreshed by rain, remind us of those years
When she was mother to the stone.

Notes on On the Beach:

I wrote this after sitting on the beach at St Mawes, Cornwall. I seem to remember that the D-Day landings were a subject of national conversation at the time.

On the Beach

'At least it isn't raining', Grandma said,
As we sat upon the beach.
'Warm enough', said Grandpa,
Not given much to speech.
The children seeming happy,
Buried under shingle.
The seagulls screeching overhead
When someone found the Pringles.

Then Grandpa said, 'Did I ever tell you
About that beach, in Normandy,
In 1944?'
He never spoke before about the war.
'We thought we'd never reach that beach
As we struggled for the shore —
I can't say anymore'

The next year Grandpa died, quite peacefully.

I'm sitting on the same beach now,
Where Grandpa's memories came
Flooding back, like waves across the sand.
He spoke about another beach, another land.
The screech of shells, not gulls.
The shingle shore, so out of reach
In 1944.

Notes on St Mawes:

Watching our grandson, Josh, as he tacked his little dinghy out to the course set for that afternoon's races.

St Mawes

Under a fretful sky,
The sea not simply blue,
More a silver grey, a shimmering
Light that challenges the eye.

White sails gathering forces
Like a proud cavalry, beating
Windward to join the race.

It is to read the wind and know
The tide that will decide who wins
Who loses, who sees the feathered ripple
On the sea, that looked for sign,
Who crosses first the winning line.

Notes on New Beginnings:

It's so easy to see the extraordinary beauty of spring from a privileged standpoint. I may be fanciful, but I have tried to see things here from an alternative perspective. The challenge presented by illegal immigration is immense. What irony, then, that our immigrant birds are so valued, and they don't need a visa. But, I hear you say, they do go away again come the winter.

New Beginnings

Have you seen those tiny buds
That push off last year's leaves?
The neatly folded sails
That will unfurl in coming season's breeze.
Those looked for New Beginnings that raise
Our hopes of greening trees
And warmer days to come.

Hold on, hold on — that gentle breeze,
With smiling young on happy parent's knees.
New Beginnings? What about
Those desperate people in their overcrowded
Channel-splashed cold dinghies?
Clinging on to life, looking for a new
Beginning in a calmer world,
Where people, just like us, can think
About the coming spring,
When migrant birds are seen
And heard again to sing.

Notes on It's Just Not Cricket:

A humorous poem that makes a serious point: however many 'illegal immigrants' arrive in the UK, let us not forget they are individuals and deserve to be treated as such.

It's Just Not Cricket

Now look here chaps, this just won't do.
I got us re-elected, I got old Brexit done,
But these blighters just keep coming
When we should be having fun.

Now young Priti's at the wicket,
Her innings just begun,
But these blighters keep on coming
When she should be scoring runs.

She wants to send them somewhere warm,
Somewhere in the sun.
She knows it's just not cricket
And it's not South Kensington.

She's running out of answers
And she's running out of funds.
But the blighters keep on coming
And they're bringing all their chums.

She may be caught, she may be stumped,
But what is to be done.
Play up and play the game
And see them, one by one.

Notes on Saving the Planet:

From a newspaper report, "More people than ever are changing their lifestyles to tackle climate change." Among the top ten things consumers said they would give up are, bananas, chocolate, beer (brewed abroad) new clothes, travel abroad, mowing the lawn and smartphones. The last two seem quite sensible, but 42% said they would give up avocados — well really!

Saving the Planet

Don't eat meat, it's not a treat.
Cows burp and poo pure CO_2.

Don't buy new clothes, old ones will do.
Put up with tears and holes in shoes.

Don't go by plane, it's quite insane.
Just stay at home — you're not to blame.

The high street shops can go to hell,
With empty tills, shoplifting thrills
And nothing much to sell.

Just live in a tent, pitched up in the hills.
You'll pay no rent and there aren't any bills.

And when at last the time has come,
And you know your life is through,
There are all the things you could have done,
The things you didn't do!

Notes on April First:

Just a bit of fun, although there is a serious point here — don't believe everything you hear on the radio and TV (even on the BBC).

April First

On April 1st 1957, Mr Richard Dimbleby revealed,
In sonorous tones, and with all the authority
Of *Panorama*, that spaghetti grows on trees
In Switzerland.
People phoned the BBC to ask
If they could grow spaghetti at home. Yes,
They were told, but it must be germinated in tomato sauce.
They saw it on the TV so they knew it must be true.

On April 1st 1962, Swedish National Television told
The viewing public that the picture could be changed
From black and white to colour
By stretching a nylon stocking over the screen.
The fine mesh, said the expert,
Refracted the light and produced a colour image.
Stocking sales went through the roof.
They'd seen it on the TV so they knew it must be true.

Now some news just in —
Scientists have crossed a chicken with a dog.
A Maltese breed of dog, that's called a Maltipoo.
It has claws instead of paws and it's got a funny bark.
It's called a Cocker Poodle Do. It rises with the lark
And wakes up all the neighbours at precisely half past two.
I heard it on the radio, so would I lie to you?

Notes on A Numpty:

Written with unerring prophecy sometime before gravity had its way.

A Numpty

Our leader's a Numpty
They say at Whitehall.
With blond hair galore
He's a good egg, for sure,
But just like old humpty,
He'll fall.

They had a great party
With nibbles and all.
Boris was there
With his mane of blonde hair,
But just like old humpty
He'll fall.

But is he like Cinders
Who's off to the ball?
In private he's witty,
It's just such a pity
That much like old humpty
He'll fall.

Yes, he went to the ball,
Ugly sisters and all.
He got in a state,
Stayed up much too late
And fell from the top
Of the wall.

So all the Queen's horses
And all the Queen's men
Couldn't put Numpty
Together again.

Notes on Standing at the Gate:

My reaction to seeing images of those first refugees from Ukraine, typically mothers with young children after difficult journeys, often on foot before reaching the border, here referred to as, 'the gate'.

Standing at the Gate

I saw her standing at the gate. I asked
Her why she waited there. She cried and through
Her tears she said, "My country is being
Crucified. I've lost my home, my friends.
My husband stayed to fight." Then I saw
The child that hid behind her, the fright,
The look of sadness on her face. It was
Too much to take. I turned to go but she,
The mother, held me by the sleeve and said,
"I want you to know what it was like. Our home
Was bombed, there was rubble in the street.
Our brothers and our sons stayed there to fight,
To wave our flag, to hold the enemy's
Advance. And when we knew we must depart
We also knew that with our spirit we
Would fight, that we would win despite the stones
That fill their soldiers' hearts. Now you can go,"
She said, "and tell the world what you have heard
Me say. And ask them, if there is a God,
To go down on their knees for us and pray."

Notes on But Not from School:

Listening to the early morning news I learnt that, after a short period of latitude, the Taliban had reimposed a ban on secondary education for girls. The skylark here epitomises those qualities we admire — freedom to ascend, persistence and a determination to be heard.

But Not from School

All the Norfolk sky seemed filled with sound
As I walked home between the fields
Of springing wheat. Skylarks, looking down upon
The vibrant green. Their voices filled the air,
Insistently proclaiming they have found
And will defend their one small piece of ground.

And in Kabul today, the sad yet bright
Eyed girls are walking home, but not from school.
They walk through dusty streets with covered heads.
Sad, yet proud, so much to give. Monstrous is
This iniquity that would keep them out of sight,
Fearful of their dreams, their voice, their freedom's right.

Notes on Caught Out:

I've seen this quite a few times: a bird of prey fearlessly attacked by otherwise normally passive birds. I was relieved when the owl managed to break away and delighted when, by chance, I found myself under the tree that provided it with some respite and refuge.

Caught Out

First, I heard a clamour. Then I saw,
Close by and low
In the early morning sky,
A pair of murderous crows
Mocking a tawny owl, caught out
In broad daylight.
A Shark among the Jets. Romeo
Among the Capulets.

Mocking is a word of courtly gesture,
Born of disrespect for someone
Out of place, who doesn't fit.
A cutting comment on inappropriate
Attire. A subject for satire,
For scathing wit.

But what I saw was more than this.
The final scene from Hamlet.
These crows made carrion cries,
Their stabbing beaks the poisoned
Swords against a startled bird,
Cornered in the sky.

Then suddenly the ruffled bird,
A silent killer in the night, dropped
Away. A clever feint, escaped,
Took refuge in the nearby wood.
I followed it until I stood beneath
Its tree, enough in leaf to keep it safe.
Out of sight, until the night
Restored it to its rightful place.

All's well that ends well.

Notes on A Tree Near Here:

This is a true story and a sad one. There's not much more to say.

A Tree Near Here

There is a tree near here
That stands, close to the road.
This tree stands out, is noticed
By the driver, driving past,
For at its base there rests a vase of flowers
And a teddy bear; a vigil
To the tragedy that happened there.

What irony. You see, she left the road
And hit the tree while overdosed on Ecstasy.
This blameless tree now holds
A memory, a place insistent
That we don't forget the life lost here.
Remembered by some flowers
And a childhood teddy bear.

Notes on Nuances:

I wrote this after listening to a radio programme titled, 'The Death of Nuance'.

I try to suggest that asking the right questions is more important than leaping to a trite answer, however irritating that must be to populist politicians and manipulators of the truth on social media platforms.

Nuances

If you didn't read the title page,
Did you read the book?
What separates a sapling from a tree
A river from a brook?

Plato, to his students, said
Observe a spinning top.
You can't see that it's moving
Until it wobbles to a stop.

Who knows how many grains of sand
It takes to make a heap;
When distant dots upon a hill
Become a flock of sheep?

What moment changes night to day,
From dark to light,
From black to white, through
Countless shades of grey?

Notes on So Many Ways to Fall:

I have taken a circuitous and I hope amusing route here towards the sudden expression of an understandable anxiety.

So Many Ways to Fall

A sudden gale, a falling tide.
You've seen those stranded boats
Left lying on their side.

Falling into trouble, falling into debt.
Slipping off the high wire
Without a safety net.

Falling like a boxer, hit upon the chin.
Sinking to the mat with vacant eyes
And white, teeth-guarded grin.

Falling out of love, the falling out of friends.
Too late to take back words,
Too late to make amends.

The falling standards of the press.
Those falsehood peddling leaders
Saying more, when more means less.

I may be getting older now.
But not too old to care
About the world and all its ills
And falling down the stairs.

Notes on Love Is:

This little poem is for those fortunate enough to come through adversity and find a stronger place.

Love Is

Love is like a piece of string, loosely tied
With a lover's knot, that sort of thing.
For some it is a few kind words,
Perhaps some bling and then a ring,
That sort of thing.

But then, with some mistakes,
With some heartaches, the heart awakes.
Then stronger knot and stronger string
Make all the angels sing.
That sort of thing.

Notes on A Christmas Card:

Amongst the robins, pheasants, and carol singers, came this seemingly untypical Christmas card. It was difficult to say what the card depicted until a glance at the back revealed the subject. This poem dwells in those first moments of puzzlement. I wrote this on Christmas Eve, 2021.

A Christmas Card

Christmas cards — again. This one's
Nice, oh! here's another robin.
But what's this, a flock of dirty
Sheep, a pile of stones?

Odd subject for a Christmas card.

'Snowy Sunrise at Hessary Tor.'
No lingering evening star here,
Although the stones seem bent
In admiration of the moor.

The camels have long gone away.
Now Dartmoor ponies rub their winter
Coat against these wise old stones.
But did the shepherds stay?

Ten thousand years this strange
Nativity of passive stone has waited.
As we do, in a world
That's slow to change.

Notes on A Doggy Conundrum:

This poem proposes a possibly sensible answer to that perplexing question, "Why do dogs always bark at the postman?"

A Doggy Conundrum

Our postman's such a happy chap
He whistles in the breeze.
Even when the weather's damp
You'll see his legs and khaki shorts
Worn high above his knees.

Why is it then that my dog barks
Whenever postman calls?
Is he guarding me from all the ads,
The double glazing, latest fads,
That thump into the hall?

One day an angry neighbour called,
He lived just up the street.
But my dog seemed to like him.
He didn't bark, he wagged his tail
And even sniffed his feet.

So one gets barks, the other sniffs,
The reason Heaven knows.
But could it be that neighbour stays
Where postman comes and goes?

Notes on Haiku 2022:

Well, half a year at least. Confined to seventeen syllables with limitless possibilities.

Haiku 2022

February
Snowdrops in sunshine
Carpeting the silent wood.
Unexpected joy.

March
Hare in the stubble.
Both ears pricked for any sound
Gathered by the wind.

April
Sunlight through the trees.
A drift of bluebells holds a
Mirror to the sky.

May
Birdsong fills the air.
Blossom paints the cherry trees,
Capturing the light.

June
The scent of roses
Colouring the hedgerow briar.
Shy, amongst the green.

July
Carefully hidden
In the shadowed morning grass.
Roe deer lying still

Notes on The River Babingley:

This describes a lovely pocket of land that lies between Sandringham and Castle Rising through which this unobtrusive little chalk stream gently winds its way to the Ouse and the Wash. Norfolk rivers take their time.

The River Babingley

The Norfolk River, Babingley
Is said to rise near Flitcham.
Clear water springs, upwelling through
The chalk, fill ponds that overflow
And start its journey to the sea.

This stream of silver grey
Winds out across the marsh.
A place where romping otters play.
March hares box. A cautious fox,
From downwind, stalks its prey.

Lapwings rise, the curlews cry.
There is no urgency.
On silent wings the barn owl flies
As Babingley joins muddy Ouse,
The widening flood, the sky.

Notes on Stiffkey Marshes:

Written after canoeing with friends near the top of a spring tide, which covered the normally exposed marshes, dramatically changing the landscape.

Stiffkey Marshes

Have you seen the Stiffkey Marshes
Covered by the tide?
When sun and moon conspire to hide
This wide expanse of blushing green.

When pushing tide fills hidden muddy creeks,
The seabirds take to wing and cry
As water parts the land from sky.

That reassuring sight of land is gone.
Like Noah's flood, the eye sees nothing
But the sea.

Until the sudden falling tide is seen
To reunite the land with sky — the salty
Samphire green, the haunting curlew's cry.

Acknowledgments

My grateful thanks to Rufus Talks for his much valued editorial suggestions. To Martin Talks for his expert help with publishing and to my wife, Judy, for her kind and honest criticism.

I am indebted to all those good friends who have encouraged me to publish and to my children and grandchildren who are such an inspiration.

Produced by My Poesi
www.mypoesi.co.uk

www.ingramcontent.com/pod-product-compliance
Lightning Source LLC
Chambersburg PA
CBHW021343060726
47591CB00006B/2139